Hello!
I am a Tiger.

# Tigers are the largest cats in the world.

The largest tiger is the Siberian tiger. It can weigh over 700 pounds (320 kg).

Tigers are excellent swimmers and enjoy spending time in water.

Tigers have webbed toes that help them paddle through water easily.

Every tiger has a unique set of stripes.

# Tigers have sharp claws that come out when they hunt.

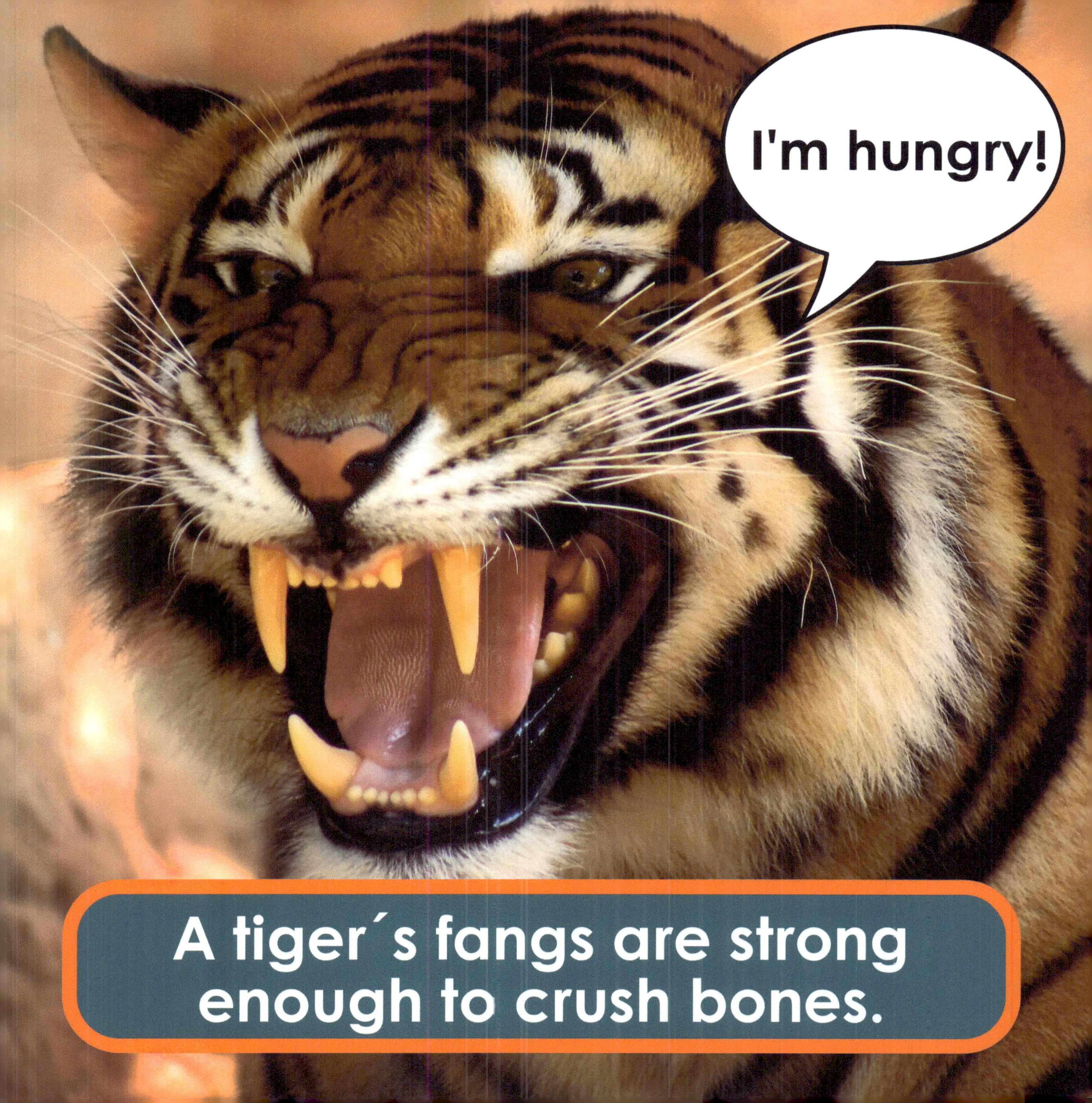


A tiger´s fangs are strong enough to crush bones.

# Tigers can eat up to 88 pounds (40 kg) of meat in one meal!

Tigers hunt large animals like deer, wild boar, and even buffalo.

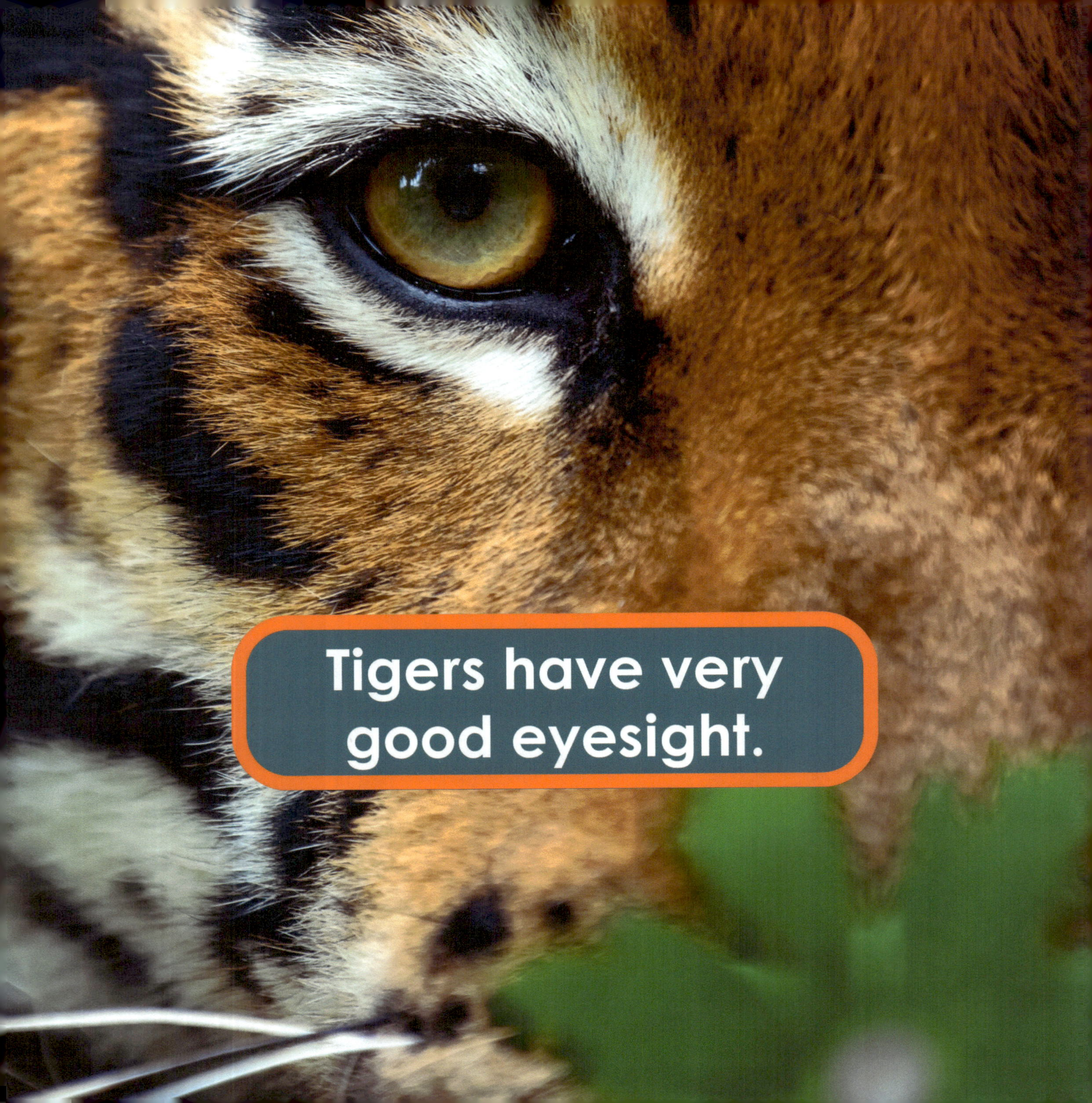

Tigers have very good eyesight.

# Tigers are incredibly fast runners!

Tigers can run up to 37 miles (60 km) per hour .

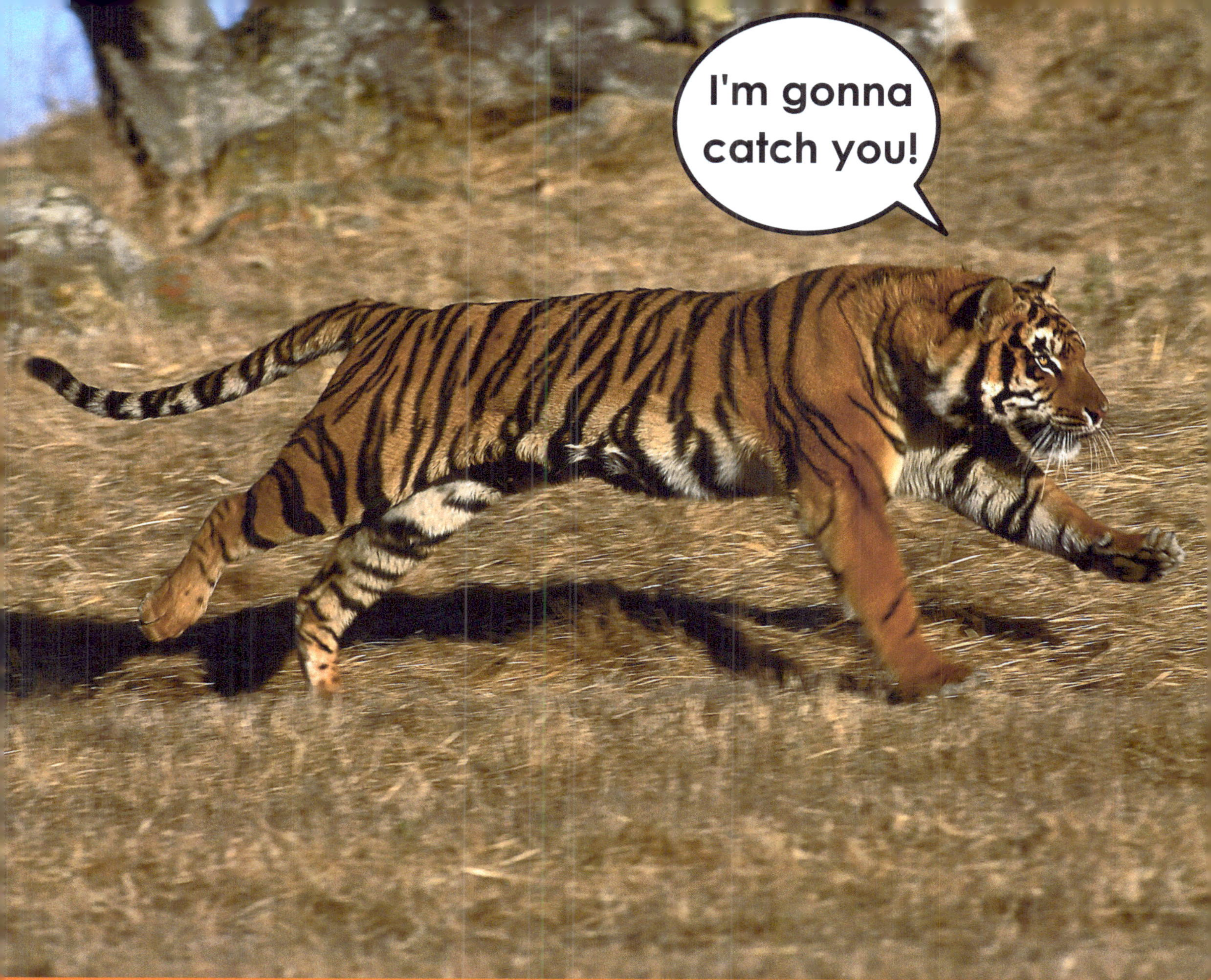


Tigers can run for short distances, but not for very long.

Tigers can jump as far as 20 feet (6 m) in a single bound.

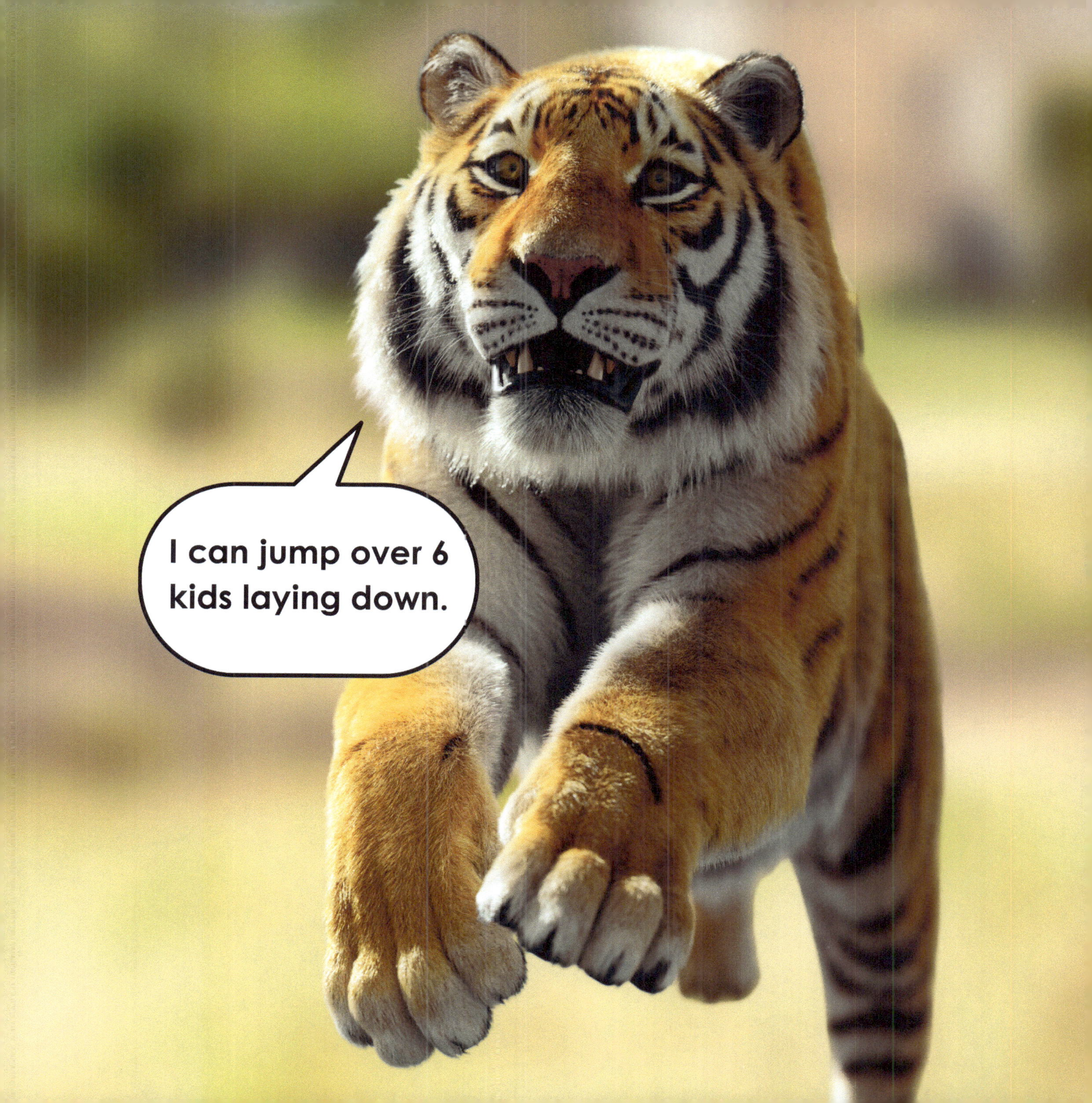
I can jump over 6 kids laying down.

# Tigers are an "endangered species".

One reason tigers are endangered is because they are losing their homes.

# Tigers are protected by laws that help save tigers from extinction.

A group of tigers is called a "streak" or an "ambush."

Tigers are usually "solitary" animals.

That means I prefer to be alone.

# Tigers mark their territory using scratch marks on trees.

They think their area is their own and they want to keep it safe from other animals.

Tigers live for 15 to 20 years.

**Tigers have large padded paws.**

You are
very loud.

You can hear a tiger's roar from about 2 miles (3 km) away.

Want more?

... and more

# Hello parents!

*scan here*

**Visit us** to find out about new releases and *FREE* offers. We'll let you know when we have a new release coming out and how you can get it for FREE.
And you can cast your vote for what book we make next!

*or visit here*

ActiveBrainsBooks.com

---

*scan here*

**Let us know what you think.** As an independent publisher, your honest reviews mean a lot to us and our business. We'd love to hear from you!

amazon.com/review/create-review/

*or visit here*

---

**FOLLOW US** on Amazon.

amazon.com/author/activebrainsbooks

## ActiveBrainsBooks.com

ACTIVE BRAINS

www.ingramcontent.com/pod-product-compliance
Lightning Source LLC
Chambersburg PA
CBHW042057040426
42447CB00003B/257